To:

_____

From:

_____

Through Christ our comfort overflows.

2 Corinthians 1:5

Stories of Comfort for a Healthy Soul

Copyright 2001 by Christine M. Anderson

ISBN 0-310-98260-X

Requests for information should be addressed to:

Inspirio, the gift group of Zondervan
Grand Rapids, Michigan 49530
http://www.inspiriogifts.com

Compiler: Christine M. Anderson
Associate Editor: Molly Detweiler
Design Manager: Amy E. Langeler
Design: Mark Veldheer
Cover photograph © Photodisc
Interior photography by Corbis Images, Photodisc, Comstock, Eyewire, and Mark Veldheer

Printed in China
01 02 03 / HK / 5 4 3 2 1

STORIES
of
COMFORT
for a
healthy soul

Compiled by

Christine M. Anderson

inspirio
The gift group of Zondervan

CONTENTS

$\mathcal{T}$ears without an audience, without someone to hear and care, leave the wounds unhealed.

LARRY CRABB

HEALING TOGETHER

Carry each other's burdens, and in this way
you will fulfill the law of Christ.

Galatians 6:2

STRANGELY COMFORTED

Donna Gassett

GOD'S WORD

> My soul is weary with sorrow;
>> strengthen me according to your word, O LORD.
>
>> *Psalm 119:28*

IT'S FIVE MONTHS now since Mother's death. A wave of loneliness comes over me as I dress half-heartedly for the women's luncheon.

Soon I find myself seated next to a young woman I know casually from church. Her smile is quick and warm. She looks even more attractive today without the usual wig—the chemotherapy has taken its toll. Closely cropped strawberry-blond hair frames her pale face in wisps.

"I've been wanting to talk to you," she says, her tone serious. As a good pastor's wife I breathe a prayer: *Lord, help me be an encouragement to her*. After all, she has every right to be serious. Her brother died recently. She's fought cancer for five years. Because of the vigorous treatments, she's had to give up her job. Her husband, who valiantly has helped assume household responsibilities, is struggling now with health problems of his own. Their two sons approach adolescent turbulence.

A large load of pain for such fragile shoulders, I think.

"I wanted to ask you...."

Lord, give me wisdom....

"I wanted to ask you how you're handling your mother's death." She goes on. "My mother died four years ago. She was my best friend, and I still miss her terribly. So I've been meaning to ask you, how are you doing?"

My throat tightens. *Who is this angel of mercy reaching out to my grief?*

"It's hard sometimes," I whisper. "My mother was my best friend, too. I shared everything with her. Joys. Sorrows...."

"I know what you mean," she responds. "Mom and I must have talked four or five times a day on the telephone. A while ago when we bought our new car, would you believe I drove to the cemetery and said, 'Mom, how do you like the new Cougar?'" She smiles sheepishly. "I know she's far better off with the Lord, but no one can ever take her place."

I nod in agreement. We're both fumbling through our purses for tissues. Lunch is served. In the restaurant the two of us are alone in a room filled with women. Strangely comforted.

GOD'S PROMISE

You will restore my life again;
from the depths of the earth
    you will again bring me up.
You will increase my honor
    and comfort me once again, O LORD.

Psalm 71:20–21

WORDS OF COMFORT

As the body of Christ, we don't exist for
ourselves but for Christ and for one another,
for a world that has lost all hope. When the
Lord restores our souls, it's only natural that
we turn to those around us who are broken
and bleeding and put an arm around them and
walk beside them.

Sheila Walsh

PRAYER

All this day, O Lord,
let me touch as many lives as possible for thee;
and every life I touch, do thou by thy
    Spirit quicken,
whether through the word I speak,
the prayer I breathe, or the life I live.

Mary Sumner

THE HOUSE OF GRACE
Richard B. Lucco

GOD'S WORD

> Let us then approach the throne of grace with confidence, so
> that we may receive mercy and find grace to help us in our
> time of need.
>
> *Hebrews 4:16*

I EXPERIENCED GRACE before I could name it. I learned it from my
grandma, Grandma Grace.

The name fit her well. Grace. It surrounded her and me when I was
with her. It was like a cool breeze on a summer evening. I couldn't see it,
but I could feel it and enjoy it.

There was nothing better than sitting in Grandma's lap. Grace's lap.
Her lap felt like it was custom-made to fit me perfectly. I would sit and
she would read, usually *Black Beauty*. I loved the story and she loved me.
So she read it over and over again. I loved the sound of her voice and the
feel of her hand as she rubbed my head. Grace's voice. Grace's hand.

I always knew I was her favorite grandchild. She made me feel
special. It wasn't until I was an adult that I realized all seven of us grand-
children felt the same way. And we were all right. Somehow, each of us
fit perfectly in her lap. Each of us was her favorite. Grace's favorite.

When I was eleven my father died. We spent an afternoon and
evening at the funeral home. Visitation, they called it. I called it dumb. I
didn't understand how folks could talk and laugh right there in front of the
casket. They said he looked good. I said he was dead. I went and hid.
Grace found me. She didn't talk. She just held me. Her tears mixed with
mine. Grace's comfort.

Thanksgiving was always at Grandma's house. Everyone sat around
the table. No separate card tables for the kids. We were a family and
somehow the table was big enough. Grace's table. One year some extra

people showed up. We made room around the table.

One night we wanted to know what would happen if she took the top off the popcorn popper. She showed us. Popcorn flew everywhere. We rolled on the floor, diving for popcorn, and laughing hysterically. Grace's joy.

My hope and prayer is that the church can be like Grandma's house. A place where people can experience grace before they can name it. A gracious space where people can know they belong. A place where they can hear grace's voice and feel grace's hand. A community where grace's comfort and grace's joy are real. A table where there is room and everyone is welcome. A grace-filled place. A gracious space.

GOD'S PROMISE

To each one of us grace has been given as Christ apportioned it.

Ephesians 4:7

WORDS OF COMFORT

You see, it was grace that was wrapped in swaddling clothes and laid in a manger. It was grace that dwelt among us, grace that healed the sick, cured the blind, and raised the dead. It was grace that partied with ragged tax collectors, grace that was called friend of sinners, grace that would not cast the first stone. It was grace that was nailed to the cross along with our sin and guilt, grace that the tomb could not hold, grace that now sits on the right hand of the Father, grace that will one day come back for you and me. When we've been there 10,000 years and every other word has been used up and worn out, we will just be starting to sing about grace.

John Ortberg

Prayer

O God, our heavenly Father, who hast commanded us to love one another as thy children, and hast ordained the highest friendship in the bond of thy Spirit, we beseech thee to maintain and preserve us always in the same bond, to thy glory, and our mutual comfort, with all those to whom we are bound by any special tie, either of nature or of choice; that we may be perfected together in that love which is from above, and which never faileth when all other things shall fail. Send down the dew of thy heavenly grace upon us, that we may have joy in each other that passeth not away; and, having lived together in love here, according to thy commandment, may live for ever together with them, being made one in thee, in thy glorious kingdom hereafter, through Jesus Christ our Lord.

John Austin

THE LAUNDROMAT
Polly Hamlin

GOD'S WORD

Love one another deeply, from the heart.

1 Peter 1:22

IT WAS A BUSY DAY at the laundromat. I was standing beside a woman who was hurriedly unloading a dryer. I noticed that she was unloading jeans and shirts and surmised she must be doing laundry for her son, since this is a college town.

I said, "Looks like you have a son in college." She turned to me and said very sharply, "I'm glad to be able to wash my son's clothing!" Then, "I wish I could still wash my daughter's clothing!"

I thought, *Uh-oh, I don't think I want to pursue this.*

I turned and walked over to the counter and stood there while she finished unloading her dryers. Questions to God were pounding through my head. "Oh, God ... do I say something ... do something ... ignore this? What should I do?"

My son, T.J., had taken his life seven years before. He was thirty-one years old and suffering from manic-depression. He had been fine until about eighteen months before his death, and then began struggling with depression. He had been admitted for treatment in the summer and after three weeks was released without any supervision. On December 4, 1990 he drove his van out to a small lake ... and took his life. We began missing him shortly after lunch when he didn't return to work. His partner in the recording studio had seen a white van at the lake near the interstate and went out to investigate, saw his body, slumped down between the seats, and called the police. He had ended his life with a shotgun.

To say this was one of the darkest hours of my life would be to minimize the situation. He was the youngest, and my only son. He was sort of the "star" of our family. I have two daughters, older than T.J. He had been a musician's musician—had his own recording studio, worked in a music store, was always involved with music. We all loved him so very much and were so proud of him.

When we lost him, it seemed for a while that my life turned very dark and very

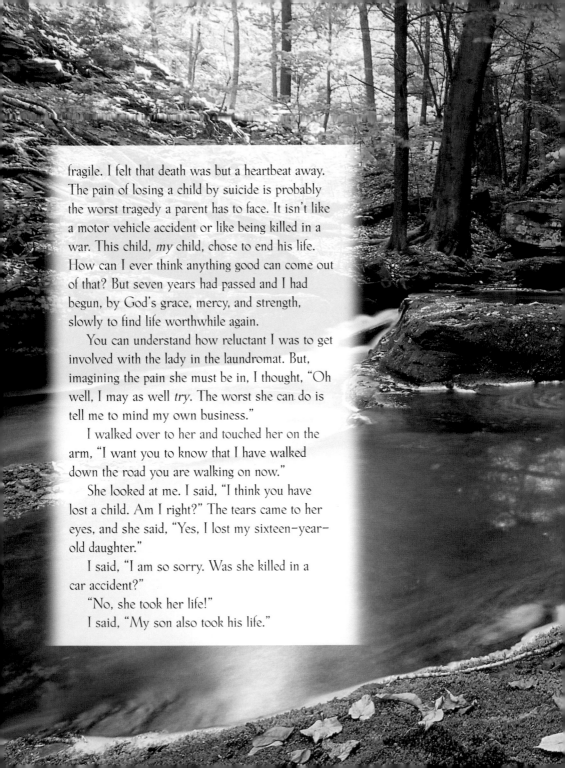

fragile. I felt that death was but a heartbeat away. The pain of losing a child by suicide is probably the worst tragedy a parent has to face. It isn't like a motor vehicle accident or like being killed in a war. This child, *my* child, chose to end his life. How can I ever think anything good can come out of that? But seven years had passed and I had begun, by God's grace, mercy, and strength, slowly to find life worthwhile again.

You can understand how reluctant I was to get involved with the lady in the laundromat. But, imagining the pain she must be in, I thought, "Oh well, I may as well *try*. The worst she can do is tell me to mind my own business."

I walked over to her and touched her on the arm, "I want you to know that I have walked down the road you are walking on now."

She looked at me. I said, "I think you have lost a child. Am I right?" The tears came to her eyes, and she said, "Yes, I lost my sixteen-year-old daughter."

I said, "I am so sorry. Was she killed in a car accident?"

"No, she took her life!"

I said, "My son also took his life."

Then she began to tell me how she had found her daughter, dead, in the living room of their home after coming back from shopping. The daughter was an anorexic and had been in treatment. They thought she was recovering. The tears began to flow from both of us. I reached out and took her in my arms. It seemed that we were the only people in the laundromat. She talked and talked as if a dam had broken.

Listening to this mother's story, I assured her that she would receive comfort from the God of all comfort. As she dried her tears, she said softly, "I believe that God put you here for me today."

She wrote to me often after that and I always wrote back to her. I never, *ever*, told her, "This is what you should do ..." I just let her tell me how she was feeling—all the anger, bitterness, doubts, fears, emptiness, *all* of it—because she knew that I understood exactly what she was telling me.

There is a price to pay for getting involved. After my encounter with her I began to cry a lot more, remember a lot more, but I knew that God would hold both of us. God's strength, indeed, is made perfect in weakness.

WORDS OF COMFORT

Suffering prepares us to comfort others.
Words from smiling, indifferent faces to
wounded hearts mean little; but words from a
fellow sufferer support and uplift. Suffering
removes artificial props of security and resets
the stage of our personal world with new
dependence on Christ. We cannot change the
circumstance. We must trust God. As Jesus
entrusted himself to the Father on the
torture–rack of the cross, so we too entrust
ourselves to our Savior.

Charles Stanley

GOD'S PROMISE

Praise be to the God and Father of our Lord
Jesus Christ, the Father of compassion and
the God of all comfort, who comforts us in
all our troubles, so that we can comfort those
in any trouble with the comfort we ourselves
have received from God.

2 Corinthians 1:3–4

PRAYER

Give me, Lord, a stout heart to bear my own
burdens, a tender heart to bear the burdens of
others, and a believing heart to lay all my
burdens on you, for you care for us.

Lesslie Newbigin

WHEN COMFORT COMES
Bonnie R. Stevens

GOD'S WORD

Dear friends, since God so loved us, we also ought to love one another. No one has ever seen God; but if we love one another, God lives in us and his love is made complete in us.

1 John 4:11–12

MY MOTHER DIED on a Sunday. She died in church while Dad was reading the Scripture lesson. I was in the choir on the platform following along in the pew Bible when Dad stopped talking. At first I looked up, startled that he had stopped, concerned that something was wrong with him. Then I saw what had interrupted my father's reading. One of the ushers was carefully carrying my mother out of the church, across the street, and into the parsonage. A heart attack had quietly ended her life.

I was in my early twenties, the youngest of three. Her death was my first experience of losing a loved one. My mother was a positive person, kind, thoughtful, full of laughter, and a true servant for Christ. I loved her dearly.

We decided to have visitation at the funeral home on the following Friday and a memorial service the next day, Saturday. It was a long week. I chose to stay at home to be with my dad. On Wednesday night, choir rehearsal night, Dad and I thought some of the choir members might stop by the house either before or after rehearsal. We prepared coffee and a plate of cookies. Dad sat in the big green chair, pretending to read the newspaper, while I sat at the end of the long sofa staring into space. We heard the cars arriving at the church across the street. The doorbell did not ring but Dad reasoned, "That's okay. They have to be on time for rehearsal. They'll come here after."

At nine o'clock we heard car doors slamming and our hope for company ended as the cars drove away. My father was stoic and practical. "It's late," he said, "people need to get home. Let's wash up the dishes." How we longed for company, for companionship, in our grief.

It was a relief on Friday when the relatives began arriving. The visitation time at the funeral home brought hundreds of people, giving hugs, sharing stories; paying their respects to a woman they held in high esteem. I was comforted by the stories, comforted by the hugs, comforted by sharing tears and laughter. I was even comforted by the fact that so many people showed up. It confirmed what I already knew—that my mother was someone very special.

The memorial service on Saturday was filled to overflowing. Those of us in the family cried through the Scripture and the music, but I remember being filled with gratitude that I had a mother who was so well loved.

Later, when only relatives remained at the house, we enjoyed a meal together, gathering around the dining room table to once again share stories. I was so happy that my aunts and uncles were there. Just their presence was a comfort to me.

My first experience of loss taught me an important lesson: the company of family and friends eases the pain of grief. I can't remember a single word that anyone said; I just remember that the comfort came when the people came.

WORDS OF COMFORT

But don't we have enough pain of our own without taking on the pain of others? Herein lies a grand illusion, for there is no such thing as "pain of our own."… Suffering is communal. Like love it can only be shared. If we are to share people's joys we must also share their sorrows. Shrinking from sorrow, we shrink from joy as well.

Mike Mason

GOD'S PROMISE

Our hope for you is firm, because we know that just as you share in our sufferings, so also you share in our comfort.

2 Corinthians 1:7

PRAYER

And now as we pray to you,
Help us to believe in your love,
so that we may be certain
that you will hear our prayer;
Help us to believe in your power,
so that we may be certain
that you are able to do for us
above all that we ask or think;
Help us to believe in your wisdom,
so that we may be certain
that you will answer,
not as our ignorance asks,
but as your perfect wisdom knows best.
All this we ask through Jesus Christ our Lord. Amen.

William Barclay

SANCTUARY

Joanna Bloss

GOD'S WORD

O God, you are my God;
> earnestly I seek you.
My soul thirsts for you;
> my body longs for you
in a dry and weary land
> where there is no water.
I have seen you in your sanctuary
> and beheld your power and your glory.
Because your love is better than life,
> my lips will glorify you.

Psalm 63:1–3

EARLY ONE SUNNY and already hot August morning, my husband, Rob, and I kissed our three children goodbye. We were headed to the city, first for a sonogram to evaluate the condition of our baby, with whom I was five months pregnant, then to celebrate our tenth anniversary with lunch and maybe a movie.

I was eager to get the sonogram out of the way. An earlier blood test had indicated there might be a problem and we were hoping the test would give us good news.

We arrived at the medical office and a technician escorted us to a dark room where she squeezed cold jelly onto my abdomen. I've had my share of sonograms, yet it never ceases to amaze me, this miraculous glimpse inside my womb. The technician navigated her way through the baby's vital organs, pointing out the bladder, the kidneys, the spinal cord. Suddenly she was quiet, and excused herself from the room. At that instant, my husband knew. I did not.

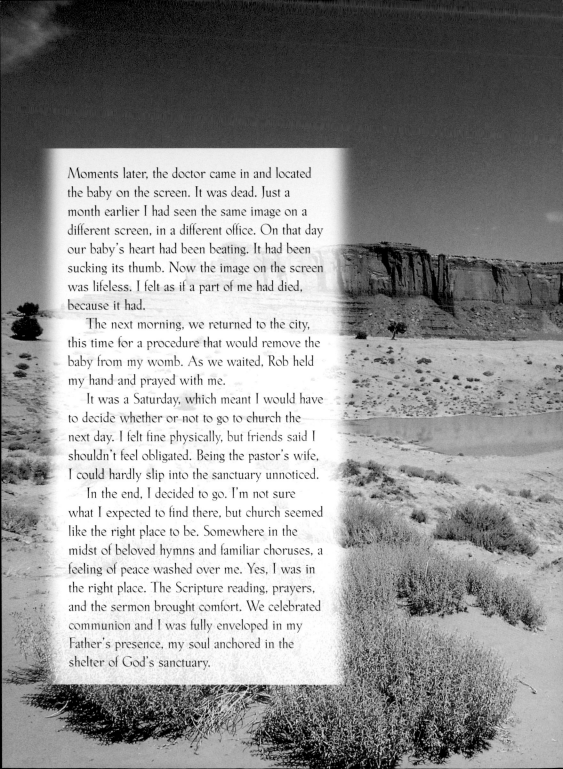

Moments later, the doctor came in and located the baby on the screen. It was dead. Just a month earlier I had seen the same image on a different screen, in a different office. On that day our baby's heart had been beating. It had been sucking its thumb. Now the image on the screen was lifeless. I felt as if a part of me had died, because it had.

The next morning, we returned to the city, this time for a procedure that would remove the baby from my womb. As we waited, Rob held my hand and prayed with me.

It was a Saturday, which meant I would have to decide whether or not to go to church the next day. I felt fine physically, but friends said I shouldn't feel obligated. Being the pastor's wife, I could hardly slip into the sanctuary unnoticed.

In the end, I decided to go. I'm not sure what I expected to find there, but church seemed like the right place to be. Somewhere in the midst of beloved hymns and familiar choruses, a feeling of peace washed over me. Yes, I was in the right place. The Scripture reading, prayers, and the sermon brought comfort. We celebrated communion and I was fully enveloped in my Father's presence, my soul anchored in the shelter of God's sanctuary.

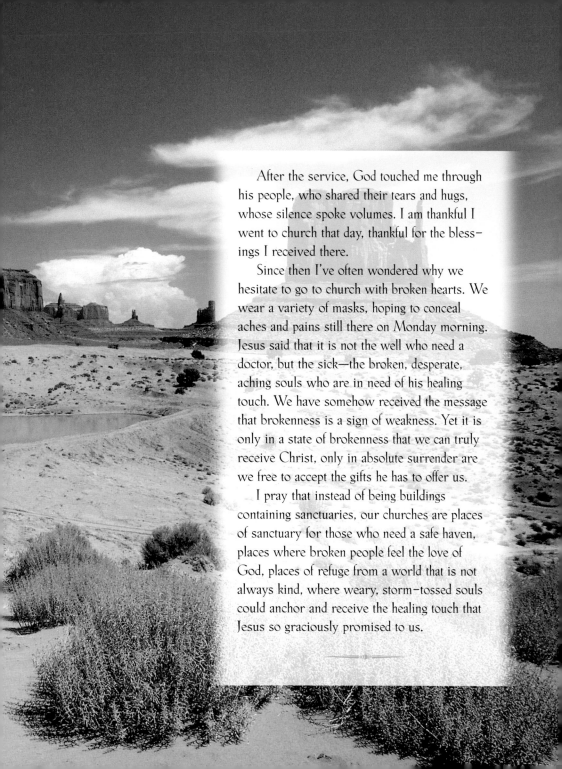

After the service, God touched me through his people, who shared their tears and hugs, whose silence spoke volumes. I am thankful I went to church that day, thankful for the blessings I received there.

Since then I've often wondered why we hesitate to go to church with broken hearts. We wear a variety of masks, hoping to conceal aches and pains still there on Monday morning. Jesus said that it is not the well who need a doctor, but the sick—the broken, desperate, aching souls who are in need of his healing touch. We have somehow received the message that brokenness is a sign of weakness. Yet it is only in a state of brokenness that we can truly receive Christ, only in absolute surrender are we free to accept the gifts he has to offer us.

I pray that instead of being buildings containing sanctuaries, our churches are places of sanctuary for those who need a safe haven, places where broken people feel the love of God, places of refuge from a world that is not always kind, where weary, storm-tossed souls could anchor and receive the healing touch that Jesus so graciously promised to us.

WORDS OF COMFORT

Everything in spiritual community is reversed
from the world's order. It is our weakness,
not our competence, that moves others; our
sorrows, not our blessings, that break down
the barriers of fear and shame that keep us
apart; our admitted failures, not our paraded
successes that bind us together in hope.

Larry Crabb

GOD'S PROMISE

"I will turn their mourning into gladness.
I will give them comfort and joy instead of
sorrow," says the LORD.

Jeremiah 31:13

PRAYER

Lord Jesus Christ,
Son of the Living God,
Comforter of widows,
Washer of feet,
Show us how to care for each other.
Teach us to love as you did:
Unconditionally, unilaterally,
Without fear or favour,
Pride or prejudice.
Give us open hearts and wise minds
And hands that are worthy
To serve in your name.

Sheila Cassidy

The secret of waiting is the faith that the seed has been planted, that something has begun. Active waiting means to be present fully to the moment, in the conviction that something is happening where you are and you want to be present to it. A waiting person is someone who is present to the moment, who believes that this moment is *the* moment.

A waiting person is a patient person. The word "patience" means the willingness to stay where we are and live the situation out to the full in the belief that something hidden there will manifest itself to us.

HENRI J.M. NOUWEN

WAITING
for
ANSWERS

Wait for the LORD;
be strong and take heart and wait for the LORD.

Psalm 27:14

GOD IS AWAKE
Sheila Walsh

GOD'S WORD

Awake, O LORD!
Rise up and help us;
redeem us because of your unfailing love.

Psalm 44:23, 26

MOST DAYS I AM HAPPY to be alive. Many days drift along in sameness. But sometimes there are days like today when my heart is heavy and sad; I have a dear friend who is in trouble.

From the day she was born it seemed as if the nails were driven into her soul. Her birth mother and father decided not to raise her; she was surrendered for adoption. That would be a gift for some who find love and a real family in the loving arms of people who have prayed for such a miracle. But the home she was placed into was not a safe place. She was sexually and physically abused from the age of five, and in her early teens she turned to prostitution and a life on the streets.

There, for the first time, she had a family. The other kids on the streets took her in and cared for her. She found a place to belong. Drugs and alcohol took some of the edge off the filth and some of the cold out of the nights.

One day a girl walked up to her and asked if she knew that Jesus loved her. She laughed. Amidst the abuse, her adoptive mother had preached to her about adhering to the laws of the Bible—if she didn't, her mother said, she would roast in hell. But something in her cried out to believe that somewhere there could be a God who loved her. So she wandered into a church and prayed to be accepted into God's family. It wasn't easy to break away from the life she had known. It wasn't easy to walk away from her street family, particularly since everyone in her new Christian family seemed so busy, but she had courage and she set her face to loving God.

We've known each other for about seven years. She wrote to me when I was co-host of "The 700 Club," and over time we became good friends. I need her in my life. She is honest and kind, and she tells me when I am full of hot air.

Life has not become any easier for her. She has life-threatening health problems. She has been institutionalized for depression in a state hospital, where they kept her so doped up that she was like a vegetable. Through it all she has tried so hard to keep living for Christ.

Today she told me that she can't do it anymore. As one disaster follows another, she is tired of trying to be hopeful about her life. She wants to end it now. She is not trying to manipulate me or make me feel sorry for her. She is just being herself, telling me the truth: "I can't take this anymore." We talked for an hour and she promised me that she would not do anything today.

I called her tonight; she is being admitted to a state mental hospital on a "seventy-two-hour hold." When she had to hang up because the hospital attendant was there to pick her up, I felt so desperate, so angry. I don't understand why her life has to be like this. Why is it that some people find flowers everywhere they turn, and others are stung every time they reach out their hands? We prayed together on the phone, tears pouring down our faces. I know that she is afraid. She has told me before that she would rather die than go back to one of those places.

I read that despair cuts us off from mercy. But sometimes mercy seems so slow to come. I know that we are promised that we will not be given more than we can bear. But I look at my friend and that doesn't seem true. I have such an ache in my soul that I don't know what to do with myself. So I sit here at my computer and write until I can go and see her. I walk around my house and I cry out to God. I remind him in my broken arrogance of all the things that he has promised. I tell him, as if he has forgotten, that he has a very scared daughter who is locked away tonight, who needs him. And even as I write I am reminded that my ache for my friend does not hold a candle to the relentless compassion of Christ. They won't let me into her ward tonight, but they can't keep him out.

When emotions beat against our souls like wave after wave in the worst of a storm, there is nowhere to turn but to Christ. As I sit for a while and think about him, I hear the loneliest words in the world: "Jesus cried out in a loud voice, '*Eloi, Eloi, lama sabachthani?*—which means, 'My God, my God, why have you forsaken me?'" (Matthew 27:46). On that brutal tree Christ embraced total isolation so that you and I never have to be alone. I am learning that that doesn't mean that life will be free of pain; it means that in the midst of the darkest night, he comes walking. Along the bleakest hospital corridors, he comes walking. When you think that the world has left you all alone, listen closely, he comes walking.

WORDS OF COMFORT

Trust is confidence in the character of God. Firmly and deliberately you say, "I do not understand what God is doing or even where God is, but I know that he is out to do me good." This is trust. This is how to wait.

Richard J. Foster

GOD'S PROMISE

God who watches over you will not slumber;
indeed, he who watches over Israel
   will neither slumber nor sleep.

Psalm 121:3–4

PRAYER

God, I want so much to trust you, but the weight—and the wait—of unanswered questions feels like a millstone of doubt around my neck and I am sinking fast. I need you. In the stormy sea of things I do not understand, buoy the thrashing limbs of my faith. For every pressing question, help me to trust that your unfailing love is answer enough for now.

Marie Carlson

PLEASE HEAL ME!

Joni Fareckson Tada

GOD'S WORD

Take a new grip with your tired hands and stand firm on your
shaky legs. Mark out a straight path for your feet. Then those who
follow you, though they are weak and lame, will not stumble and
fall but will become strong.

Hebrews 12:12–13 (NLT)

THE YEAR IS 1967. I am seventeen years old, stuck, paralyzed on a
Stryker frame in a state institution. Yet even the dark shadowed room
can't match the black cloud hanging over me. I am desperate, looking for
a miracle. What young girl lying numb and motionless with tubes
running in and out of her wouldn't? "Oh God, will you please heal me?"
I whispered, crying in the night.

It was the first time I felt I had the faith to pray for a miracle. My
prayer had been prompted by a friend who, earlier in the day, had sat by
my bedside and read John 5:2–9:

"Now there is in Jerusalem near the Sheep Gate a pool, which in
Aramaic is called Bethesda and which is surrounded by five
covered colonnades. Here a great number of disabled people
used to lie—the blind, the lame, the paralyzed. One who was
there had been an invalid for thirty-eight years. When Jesus
saw him lying there and learned that he had been in this condition for a long time, he asked him, 'Do you want to get well?'…
Then Jesus said to him, 'Get up! Pick up your mat and walk.'
At once the man was cured; he picked up his mat and walked."

It was the part about being an invalid for thirty-eight years that got
me. *Please Lord, I can't live without use of my hands or legs for three
days, let alone thirty years. I'm not like that man by the pool at Bethesda.
Be compassionate to me, like you were to him. Heal me!*

I imagined myself among the many when Jesus walked by the pool. I saw the columns and tiled porches. There I was, lying on a straw mat, Jesus' eyes meeting mine, him sensing my desperation, stepping over others to kneel by my mat, reaching down in compassion, touching my cheek and— yes!—saying, "Daughter, be healed." The power of the image caused a muscle spasm, and my body shook in anticipation. *Oh, God, yes, I believe you want to heal me. I believe! Raise me up, I ask you, put me in the pool, too!* I strained to rise from my Stryker. My legs and hands never got the message.

The year is 1998. I abandoned long ago those desperate times of prayer, those urgent leadings that Jesus might heal me, too, like the man at the Pool of Bethesda.

And suddenly, I'm here—at the actual pool. Ken and I are vacationing in Israel, touring Jerusalem, and unexpectedly as we turn a corner ... here's the pool! Here are the ruins of the five colonnades. In my mind's eye I see hundreds of sick and paralyzed people. I turn to Ken and say, "You wouldn't believe how many times I used to picture myself here ..." I scan the ruins and murmur, "And now, after thirty years, I'm ... here."

Tears well in my eyes. "I made it," I say weakly, resting my arm on the guardrail. "Jesus didn't pass me by. He didn't overlook me. He answered my prayer: He said, 'No.'"

And I'm glad. A 'no' answer has purged sin from my life, strengthened my commitment to him, forced me to depend on grace, bound me with other believers, produced discernment, fostered sensitivity, disciplined my mind, taught me to spend my time wisely, stretched my hope, made me know Christ better, helped me long for truth, led me to repentance of sin, goaded me to give thanks in times of sorrow, increased my faith, and strengthened my character. Being in this wheelchair has meant knowing *him* better, feeling *his* strength every day.

The noon sun is high and hot, and a brisk wind dries my tears. The quiet moment becomes a milestone, an altar of remembrance. The Lord brought me here that I might thank him for the wiser choice, the better answer, the richer path. "And, Lord," I say out loud, gazing at the dusty, bare porticos and imagining them crowded with the many that day who did not get healed, "thank you for giving me the chance to tell others that sometimes 'no' is a better answer. Sometimes healing happens on the inside."

"Are you okay?" Ken touches my cheek.

"Yes," I sniff and laugh. I can't believe that I'm crying and laughing at the same time. There are more important things in life than walking.

WORDS OF COMFORT

Wait for God, even if the night seems dark. He will give you everything you need when you need it. It may not be what you want or expect, but it is the best.

Peter Wallace

GOD'S PROMISE

The LORD longs to be gracious to you;
    he rises to show you compassion.
For the LORD is a God of justice.
    Blessed are all who wait for him!

Isaiah 30:18

PRAYER

Almighty and merciful God, who art the strength of the weak, the refreshment of the weary, the comfort of the sad, the help of the tempted, the life of the dying, the God of patience and of all consolation; thou knowest full well the inner weakness of our nature, how we tremble and quiver before pain, and cannot bear the cross without thy divine help and support. Help me, then, O eternal and pitying God, help me to possess my soul in patience, to maintain unshaken hope in thee, to keep that childlike trust which feels a Father's heart hidden beneath the cross; so shall I be strengthened with power according to thy glorious might, in all patience and long-suffering; I shall be enabled to endure pain and temptation, and, in the very depth of my suffering, to praise thee with a joyful heart.

Johann Habermann

to health? It would have been the miracle of the century! At first I would have said yes, and I often prayed for this. Eventually, I had other thoughts. Such a miracle would have lifted us into a lonely spiritual stratosphere where we would have become a source of confusion and envy to those who suffer and die with no miraculous intervention. Margaret's miraculous restoration can wait until resurrection morning when it will be shared with all God's sleeping saints!

After Margaret had breathed her last, I stood by her bedside and looked at her face, sagging and distorted, and at her tortured body, twisted by the pain she had suffered. I knew, of course, that we would some day be reunited by the resurrection, but her resurrection was not now on my mind. I was aware only of my love for the Margaret who had just left me. It occurred to me that I would be able to perform one last loving act for her. I replaced her dentures and straightened her face and held it until it stayed. Then I straightened her knees and laid her arms by her sides. Now she looked like the Margaret who had been my loving companion for over six decades.

I kissed her lips, still warm from the life that had once been so vibrant. For the last time I said, "Good night, sweetheart," and I left her body with the professionals to prepare for burial, and her spirit with the Savior to carry to the sunrise. I had walked with her into the darkness as far as I could go.

Though there had been no miracle healing, I was at peace with God. I was content with the greatest miracle of all—the miracle of the God who so loved that he gave.

WORDS OF COMFORT

What we need to know, of course, is not just that God exists, not just that beyond the steely brightness of the stars there is a cosmic intelligence of some kind that keeps the whole show going, but that there is a God right here in the thick of our day-by-day lives who may not be writing messages about himself in the stars but in one way or another is trying to get messages through our blindness as we move around down here knee-deep in the fragrant muck and misery and marvel of the world. It is not objective proof of God's existence that we want but the experience of God's presence. That is the miracle we are really after, and that is also, I think, the miracle that we really get.

Frederick Buechner

GOD'S PROMISE

May your unfailing love be my comfort, O LORD,
     according to your promise.

Psalm 119:76

PRAYER

Dear Lord, it seems that you are so madly in love with your creatures that you could not live without us. So you created us; and then, when we turned away from you, you redeemed us. Yet you are God, and so have no need of us. Your greatness is made no greater by our creation; your power is made no stronger by our redemption. You have no duty to care for us, no debt to repay us. It is love, and love alone, which moves you.

Catherine of Siena

imitate him by being loving and obedient. Then one day when I was twelve, a church deacon came to our house and began reading, "For all have sinned ..." (Romans 3:23). For the first time I understood that, no matter how good I tried to be, I was, by nature, hopelessly evil. Then the deacon continued, "While we were still sinners, Christ died for us" (Romans 5:8). Suddenly I could picture Jesus hanging on the cross, taking my punishment. In that moment, I was so overwhelmed by the magnitude of his love that I couldn't even pray. All I could do was weep with sorrow and repentance. I gave Jesus my whole heart.

I spent my teenage years defending my faith to my father. He railed about an uncaring God who thought nothing of squashing us like ants and who liked to "watch us bring trouble on ourselves and laugh." Daddy's jibes drove me to study Scripture and to forge a foundation for my faith. Later, when others abandoned their beliefs to challenges by college professors, my faith stood firm, having been strengthened through prolonged debate with my father.

I was living in another state when he died. My mother could offer no comforting stories of deathbed conversion. He had, in fact, bled to death on the operating table with no counselors at all. No notes or diary miraculously appeared to indicate a private communion with the Lord. Nothing of substance provided a hook upon which I could fasten any hope about his eternal destiny.

The pastor who preached the funeral spoke of life, but as the casket descended into the grave, I could see only death. As they put my father into the ground, I could not find comfort in thoughts of a joyful reunion in heaven; I could not envision a smiling God welcoming his child home. My father had left me only his agnostic past. The weight was beyond words, tears, or prayer. I felt utterly abandoned.

The day after the funeral, I found an empty little church where I knew no one and went in to pray. In my agony I could not express trust or hope or find strength in any remembered Scripture. All I could do was cry out, "But, Lord, I loved him so much!" In the depths of my heart, I heard my Savior answer clearly, gently, "Don't you think I loved him, too?"

What a magnificent release! I suddenly realized that, as much as I had desired eternal life for my father, his Father had desired it infinitely more. God would have known the words to speak to Daddy in the moments before his death, with or without a human instrument. I didn't know my father's response, but I knew that I could trust him to the God who had loved him all of his life and who knew him more intimately than anyone on earth.

In the twenty-five years since my father's death, the once-sharp pain has become a dull ache, but the despair never has returned. He had only this lifetime in which to accept or reject Christ and salvation, and I honestly do not know what his choice was. I still miss his presence, but I have learned to leave the difficult questions to the Lord.

"We live by faith, not by sight" (2 Corinthians 5:7). That faith is not based in the surety of happy endings, but in the God of justice, mercy, and indescribable love. My faith is not that the answer will be according to my desire, but that the one who gives the answer is right.

WORDS OF COMFORT

In times of darkness, our Lord shares the darkness with his disciple. He is there. He knows all about it. There must be a sense of mystery, for mystery requires you to be guided by someone who knows more than you do. This is true, both physically and spiritually speaking. Never forget this fact.

Oswald Chambers

GOD'S PROMISE

You, O LORD, keep my lamp burning;
my God turns my darkness into light.

Psalm 18:28

PRAYER

Almighty God, who in thy wisdom hast so ordered our early life that we ... must walk by faith and not by sight; grant us such faith in thee that, amidst all things that pass our understanding, we may believe in thy fatherly care, and ever be strengthened by the assurance that underneath are the everlasting arms; through Jesus Christ our Lord.

Source unknown

THE BIRDHOUSE

Philip Gulley

GOD'S WORD

"Forget the former things;
    do not dwell on the past.
See, I am doing a new thing!" says the LORD.

Isaiah 43:18–19

A FRIEND OF MINE has a serene office with rocking chairs and windows on two sides that look out into woods. The windows have screens. In warm weather he opens the windows and listens to the birds. Once when I was visiting him, I noticed a weathered birdhouse hanging on his wall.

"Why do you have a birdhouse in your office?" I asked him.

"That was my grandfather's," he told me. Then he told me how it came to hang on his wall.

The story began in 1949 in a little southern Indiana town. It was a Sunday morning in early June. My friend's Aunt Betty had just graduated from high school. Betty and her family attended the Baptist church, where they were singing the opening hymn one Sunday when Betty noticed a handsome young man across the aisle. He was a traveling Baptist, passing through on business. She knew nothing about him, but by the third verse had fallen in love with his strong jaw. Two weeks later she went away with him, and they were married.

A year later the traveling Baptist left her, and Betty returned home with a baby girl. Her father went to the train station to pick them up and drive them home. Betty sobbed the whole way; her tears rained down on her baby. Her daddy told her, "You're always welcome to stay with us. Your mother and I still love you. You know that, don't you?"

The next Sunday, he took Betty and his little granddaughter back to church, and when people whispered about them, he stood tall, daring anyone to look crossways at them. When the preacher talked against divorced people and pointed fingers, Betty's father reached over and put his arm around his daughter and drew her close.

"My grandfather was a wonderful man," my friend told me. "He took in his little granddaughter, and he loved her as his own."

From the first moment he saw her in his daughter's arms at the train station, he became a father to [his granddaughter]. He taught her how to swim at Dewart Lake and how to swing a bat and pitch a ball so no one could hit it. He taught her the kinds of things fathers teach their daughters. Then he came down with cancer. He spent his last spring on the back porch. His granddaughter sat with him. He was sixty-five and she was twelve. He was wrapping things up; she was just getting started. They sat on the back porch and listened to the birds. He taught her their songs.

One day in early May, she said, "Grandpa, let's go to town and buy a bird-house." They walked down to Fleming's Hardware and bought a birdhouse shaped like a log cabin and hung it from the back porch eaves and watched a wren build her nest and hatch her young.

That birdhouse was the last thing he ever bought. He died a month later. Today it hangs in my friend's office. He looks at it and remembers how a man opened his arms to a hurting daughter and her little baby, how he went to church and stood tall in the face of gossip and drew his daughter close when the stares grew hard. He died when my friend was one year old. He doesn't remember anything about his grandfather. All that he has from him is one birdhouse and the stories others tell about him.

His Aunt Betty remarried. She is seventy years old now and an elder in that same Baptist church, the first female elder they've ever had. Whenever young people in the church divorce, she ministers to them. She visits them in their homes and tells them, "We still love you. You know that, don't you?" She takes them back to church, and if other people look hard at them, she stands tall and puts her arm around them and draws them close.

One time the preacher got to talking about divorce and naming names. The next day Betty paid him a visit in his office and told him a little story about a young woman fresh out of high school in 1949, who fell in love with a young man and went away to get married, and how, to her deep shame and sorrow, it didn't work out. She's felt guilty about it ever since. People still talk about it. "Maybe," she told the preacher, "instead of pointing fingers, you can encourage these young people who have had their lives torn apart. Maybe you can help them put their homes back in order instead of pointing out the disrepair." The preacher listened and learned.

I listened to this story on an early summer day while sitting in my friend's office. I rocked back and forth and thought on the vagaries of self-control, and how it is that God redeems even a hasty decision made back in 1949. I considered how God has salvaged my many failures, how God has met me at my places of shame, how he's drawn me close and helped me stand tall. One more Father doing the best he can by his child.

WORDS OF COMFORT

Whatever our failings may be, we need not
lower our eyes in the presence of Jesus....
Jesus comes not for the super-spiritual but for
the wobbly and the weak-kneed who know they
don't have it all together, and who are not too
proud to accept the handout of amazin' grace.
As we glance up, we are astonished to find the
eyes of Jesus open with wonder, deep with
understanding, and gentle with compassion.

Brennan Manning

GOD'S PROMISE

God did not appoint us to suffer wrath but to
receive salvation through our Lord Jesus Christ.

1 Thessalonians 5:9

PRAYER

Christ our companion,
you came not to humiliate the sinner
    but to disturb the righteous.
Welcome us when we are put to shame,
but challenge our smugness,
that we may truly turn from what is evil,
and be freed even from our virtues,
in your name.

Janet Morley

DELIVERY SERVICE
Liz Curtis Higgs

GOD'S WORD

Help us, O God our Savior,
> for the glory of your name;
deliver us and forgive our sins
> for your name's sake.

Psalm 79:9

THE TRUTH IS, I didn't always trust in God. Despite my parents' best efforts to raise a wholesome, small-town girl, I veered off track in my mid-teens and started hanging out with a faster crowd.

First, it was sneaking a cigarette out of Mom's purse. Then, it was cutting school for an hour, then an afternoon, then a whole day. I smoked my first joint on our senior class trip. Most of the kids took the bus to New York City—I "flew." A decade-long love affair with pot began, ironically, on the steps of the Statue of Liberty.

By my twentieth birthday, I was spending four and five nights a week on a bar stool, Southern Comfort in my glass and longing in my eyes. I found companionship in many but comfort in none.

As a radio personality, I traveled "town to town, up and down the dial" through my twenties, including a stint at a hard rock station in Detroit, where shock-jock Howard Stern did mornings and I did the afternoon show. As a one-sentence summary of how low my values had plummeted, even Howard once shook his head and said, "Liz, you've got to clean up your act!"

By the fall of 1981, I found myself in Louisville, Kentucky, playing oldies at an AM station and playing dangerous games with marijuana, speed, cocaine, alcohol, and a promiscuous lifestyle. I'm one of those people who had to go all the way down to the bottom of the pit before I was forced to look up for help.

COME HOME
Sheila Walsh

GOD'S WORD

> I have wandered away like a lost sheep, O LORD;
> Come and find me.
>
> *Psalm 119:176 (NLT)*

ONE OF MY MOST treasured books is *Beside the Bony Brier Bush* by Ian Maclaren. I love the stories told in true Scottish brogue—seven stories, all with a message of deep spiritual truth. But the story that I go back to over and over again is about Lachlan Campbell and his daughter Flora.

Lachlan was a hard man, a devout believer who held the scales of justice tightly with little mercy or grace. One evening he brought a case of discipline before the church board. A young girl, he explained, had left home for the evils of London; she wasn't expected to be seen again. He came with a recommendation: that her name—the name of his own daughter, Flora—be struck off the church roll. The men in the fellowship were heartbroken for Lachlan. But they refused his recommendation; they would not take Flora's name off the role, saying, "In the Lord there is mercy and with him is plenteous redemption."

Lachlan stood before them in silence, and the minister took the broken man to his house. He sat Lachlan by the fire and like a father asked him to explain what had happened. Lachlan pulled out a letter from Flora in which she poured out her heart, asking her father to forgive her for running away—but she could no longer live by his strict standards. "Perhaps," she said, "if my mother had lived she would have understood me. My greatest regret, Father, is that I will never see you again in this world or the next."

"That's not the letter of a bad girl," said the minister kindly. "Just a sad one."

Lachlan got up to leave. "You won't take her name off the church role, but I've taken her name out of the family Bible."

For some time his neighbors in Crumtochty watched lonely, solitary Lachlan come and go until one woman could hold herself back no longer. Marget knocked on his door and told Lachlan that she had come in the name of the Lord to tell him that the family shame was his and not his daughter's. "Where would we be," she said, "if God had turned his back on us as you have on your own daughter?"

With those words God pierced this proud man's heart. Marget sat down with him and wrote to Flora, telling her to come home; her father was waiting for her with arms open wide. Every night as Lachlan went to bed he left a light burning in the window—in case it was the night that Flora came home.

And one night she did. It was dark as she made her way toward her father's house. She was so afraid. She knew her father and his iron principles well. Finally through the woods she saw the cottage; it was ablaze with light, and she understood. Running to the door, she was too overwhelmed to knock or speak, but her father knew she had come, because the dogs, who had never forgotten her or written her off, barked for joy. Lachlan opened the door. Though he had never kissed his daughter in all her twenty years, he gathered her in his arms and kissed her. That night they opened the family Bible together and wrote,

Flora Campbell, missed April 1873.

Found September 1873.

"Her father fell on her neck and kissed her."

Perhaps as you read these words you see yourself in Flora. In leaving her father's home for the big city, she was turning away also from his faith. I talk to many people who have lost the way home. Perhaps raised by strict, unbending parents, they throw their own faith away as they reject a standard that they feel is crushing them. My question is always the same: "Did you find what you were looking for?"

Perhaps you see yourself in Lachlan Campbell. Refusing to bend or compromise, you have written someone off. You have said, "I have no daughter. I have no son." Where would we be if God had done that to us?

If you have lost your way and you have lost hope, come home. The Father is waiting for you. It doesn't matter where you have been. All that matters is where you are going. And for those who have hardened hearts against someone, those who march on toward heaven without ever looking back, I hold up the picture of a father standing at the window, never letting the light go out. I challenge you to reach out and wait and pray and love—for today could be the day a child returns home.

Words of Comfort

If only we would turn, our God is ready to welcome us and to enfold us. If we so choose, we can make every day a homecoming, every day we can take time and turn to our God. God has never left us; if we draw near to him, he draws near to us. God is ever willing to welcome us with open arms.

David Adam

God's Promise

The Son of Man came to seek and to save what was lost.

Luke 19:10

Prayer

O Lord Jesus Christ, take us to thyself, draw us with cords to the foot of thy cross; for we have no strength to come, and we know not the way. Thou art mighty to save, and none can separate us from thy love. Bring us home to thyself, for we are gone astray. We have wandered: do thou seek us. Under the shadow of thy cross let us live all the rest of our lives, and there we shall be safe.

Frederick Temple

SOUL HEALER
Kay Arthur

GOD'S WORD

Heal me, O LORD, and I will be healed;
save me and I will be saved.

Jeremiah 17:14

I WILL NEVER FORGET the day I was saved. The night before, I'd been at a party. The only thing I remember about that night was that a man named Jim looked at me and said, "Why don't you quit telling God what you want and tell him that Jesus Christ is all you need?" His words irritated me.

"Jesus Christ is not all I need." My reply was curt. "I need a husband. I need a ... " and one by one I enumerated my needs, emphasizing each one by numbering them on my fingers. At five, I considered that I had surely proven my case, so I turned on my heels and went home.

For some time I had realized my lifestyle was unacceptable to God. My sins were obvious. Even I could not excuse them. For the first time in my life, I had seen my poverty of spirit. Although I had tried, I could not quit sinning. Nothing good dwelt in my flesh and I knew it (Romans 7:18–20).

I had made resolution after resolution to be good, to stop being immoral. Yet I gave in again and again. I finally concluded that there was no way I could ever be set free. I just wasn't strong enough spiritually to change. I knew I was sick—sick of soul. As a registered nurse I was an active participant in the healing of many bodies, but I didn't know of any doctor who could heal my soul. And heal myself? Well, it was impossible. I had tried.

After my divorce, I lived with gnawing guilt until finally my sin became an acceptable way of life. After all, how could my friends condemn me? We all lived the same way!

Some days I even thought, *if I could just be born again … have another start at life.* Then I would dream of what-could-have-been-if-only. I didn't know the term *born again* was in the Bible. Although my family was very religious, the Bible had not been a central part of my life. For the most part I didn't know what God's Word said. By this time I had lived for twenty-nine years, and no one had ever asked me when or even if I had been saved. I had never heard an invitation for salvation, nor had I realized that it isn't church membership or being good that makes us Christians.

Heaven and hell? Hell was what you made of your life here on earth. Heaven? Well, if my good deeds outweighed my bad, surely I would make it. At least that was what I was told. To be honest, I never felt that nice people were in any danger. No one around me had a burden for the lost. I had never heard a sermon on the need to witness.

When the morning of July 16, 1965, dawned, I couldn't face going to work. I called the doctor I worked for and told him I was sick, that I would see him Monday. I hung up the phone and got Tommy off to day camp. At loose ends, I decided I'd bake a cake and then take the boys camping.

Suddenly, in the middle of the kitchen, I looked at Mark, my younger son. He was so hungry for love. He clung to my apron. I choked out the words, "Momma's got to be alone for a few minutes." With that I rushed upstairs to my bedroom and threw myself on the floor beside my bed. "Oh God, I don't care what you do to me. I don't care if I never see another man as long as I live. I don't care if you paralyze me from the neck down. I don't care what you do to my two boys. Will you just give me peace?"

There beside my bed I found that there is a balm in Gilead that heals the sin-sick soul. There is a Great Physician. His name is Jehovah-rapha. But I would first come to know him as the Lord Jesus Christ, the Prince of Peace. On that day in my bedroom he applied the cross to the bitter waters of my life, and I was healed of sin's mortal wounds. I had turned to Jehovah-rapha, returning to the Shepherd and Guardian of my soul.

Only one Physician can heal the ills of our souls. Why look elsewhere?

WORDS OF COMFORT

Thou know'st he died not for himself,
nor for himself arose;
Millions of souls were in his heart,
and thee for one he chose.

Upon the palms of his pierced hands
engraven was thy name.
He for thy cleansing had prepared
his water and his flame.

Make sure thou with him art risen:
and now with him thou must go forth.
And he will lend thy sick soul health,
thy strivings might and worth.

Oswald Chambers

GOD'S PROMISE

"Peace, peace, to those far and near,"
says the LORD. "And I will heal them."

Isaiah 57:19

PRAYER

Great Physician of souls, heal me today. I am
tired and sick at heart. Forgive me for a life
lived far from you. I want the new heart you
promise, I want the clean-scrubbed soul only
you can give. Touch me with healing power
and make me fully yours. Amen.

Aileen Collins

GOOD FRIDAY

Christopher de Vinck

GOD'S WORD

> Jesus said, "Anyone who intends to come with me has to let me
> lead. You're not in the driver's seat—I am. Don't run from
> suffering; embrace it. Follow me and I'll show you how."
>
> *Luke 9:23 (MSG)*

FOR ME, GOOD FRIDAY means silence. When I was a child, my
mother and father insisted that, on this day, we children walk around the
house quietly. No TV. No radio. No record player. We were asked not
to play any games.

I remember sitting most of one particular Good Friday afternoon in
my father's small office. He was a writer and spent many days in, what
we called, the sun porch.

On that Good Friday I felt alone. I couldn't hear my sisters and
brothers. The television was silent. My sister's record player wasn't
echoing in the hallway.

I remember sitting on a large gray chair that unfolded into a bed. It
was an uncomfortable chair: lumpy and full of springs. I began counting
the pulled threads that were scattered on the back portion of the chair.

The next thing I knew, it was completely dark. I had fallen asleep and
woke up hours later with a blanket around me.

Obviously it was the middle of the night. The lights in the house
were out. No one was downstairs. I was frightened, afraid to move from
the chair or to call out for my father into the silence. Each Good Friday I
think about a little boy alone under his blanket with his cheeks pressed
against the rough surface of an old chair. I think about the darkness, and
the silence, and the blanket my father had covered me with to protect me
from the cold.

Christ endured the greatest silence and darkness on the Good Friday

WORDS OF COMFORT

We were built to count, as water is made to run downhill. We are placed in a specific context to count in ways no one else does. That is our destiny.

Our hunger for significance is a signal of who we are and why we are here, and it also is the basis of humanity's enduring response to Jesus. For he always takes individual human beings as seriously as their shredded dignity demands, and he has the resources to carry through with his high estimate of them.

Dallas Willard

GOD'S PROMISE

Jesus said, "I tell you the truth, anyone who has faith in me will do what I have been doing. He will do even greater things than these, because I am going to the Father."

John 14:12

PRAYER

God, I claim the promise that my life matters to you. I am here because you love me, and because I am loved by you my life has meaning and eternal significance. When things get hard, help me to remember that nothing can thwart your purpose for me. You are always in control. I praise you, Lord, for your goodness to me and for the gift of this, my one and only life.

Marie Carlson

THE OTHER SIDE OF THE TABLE
Patty Leno

GOD'S WORD

O my Comforter in sorrow, my heart is faint within me.

Jeremiah 8:18

OUR DAUGHTER JAMIE turned eight years old in August. When she was born she was healthy, bright, and she progressed normally for the first year of her life. But shortly after her first birthday things changed. Her muscle tone decreased. She stopped talking and walking. At eighteen months she lost the use of her hands. By age two Jamie had withdrawn into a world of her own. She responded to no one—not even me, her mother.

My husband, Garth, and I spent the next two years trying desperately to find a solution, a cure. The medical profession seemed baffled by her illness, and it was not until she was four that she was diagnosed with Rett Syndrome, a neurological disorder that affects only girls, causing severe mental and physical impairments. To me, Rett Syndrome was not just a disease. As far as I was concerned, it was a death sentence. Very little is known about this terrible condition, and there is yet no known cure.

In the midst of my deep emotional pain and anxiety, I had dinner with a woman whose thirteen-year-old daughter is physically handicapped. I watched the woman closely throughout the meal. I listened to her laugh and talk about normal, everyday kinds of things. She was full of joy and was confident concerning God's plan for her life.

I sat across from her, trying to understand. I was reeling from the pain in my heart. I felt defeated and empty and discouraged, but I wanted desperately to be where this woman sat—on the other side of the table. Everything seemed so much different where she was seated. But I didn't know how to get there. Would I ever experience her joy? Would I ever laugh again? Would the victory of Christ ever return to my heart?

Because I am a nurse I have seen many children born with physical

challenges, and I was not entirely surprised that I had a handicapped child. But I did expect God to heal her. I waited in eager anticipation for God to sweep away my pain. I couldn't imagine that God would want me to suffer as I was suffering.

I wanted to control God, but he is sovereign and cannot be controlled by anyone. He does what he knows will benefit us eternally. I realized that God was not asleep when Jamie was created. It was his hand that formed her. She is "fearfully and wonderfully made" as the psalmist declares in Psalm 139:14. God knew that Jamie would bring much pain into our lives, but he also knew the blessing she would bring.

Our precious little girl has little ability of her own, but she is an agent of God to change lives. Hardened and bitter people have been softened by this unique messenger from heaven. One young man, whose Christian life five years ago was shallow and powerless, started working with Jamie in a Sunday school. That same man recently was baptized in our church and gave a powerful testimony of his love for God. His mother told me that Jamie was God's secret weapon in changing his life.

Through my own pain I am able to empathize with people who are going through various struggles in their lives. The Father of compassion and the God of all comfort comforted me in my trouble so that I can comfort others (2 Corinthians 1:3–4).

I have seen his majesty at work. I marvel at the unfathomable depths of his grace. I am humbled by his love for me. My relationship with the Savior has been transfigured because of my pain, not in spite of it. And I am not alone in my pain. There are many who have gone before me and who walk with me who have pleaded with God for a reprieve. God does not always extract us from painful situations in life, but he does answer prayer. For now, Jamie has not been healed, but the Lord has confirmed his promise to me: "My grace is sufficient for you, my power is made perfect in weakness (2 Corinthians 12:9).

It has been six years since I sat across the table from the woman who laughed and talked so freely about her handicapped daughter. I still find myself on the wrong side of the table once in a while. The future is a bit frightening, and sometimes it overwhelms me. That experience draws me again and again to my Heavenly Father, and I pour out my heart to him in prayer. I know that God is at work in me, transforming the agony of my suffering into a demonstration of his grace. And so I wait, secure in his love, believing that my Father always knows what is best.

WORDS OF COMFORT

Our access to God supplies us with God's grace, the spiritual resources we need to transform trials into triumphs. "God did not abolish the fact of evil: he transformed it," wrote Dorothy Sayers. "He did not stop the crucifixion: he rose from the dead." We want God to solve the problems of suffering by method of substitution—give us health instead of pain, wealth instead of poverty, friendship instead of loneliness—when his approach is to use the method of transformation. He transformed Paul's weakness into strength and his suffering into glory.

Warren Wiersbe

GOD'S PROMISE

Those who suffer God delivers in their suffering;
    he speaks to them in their affliction.

Job 36:15

PRAYER

Dear Risen Lord, how hard it is to see clearly when devastating circumstances fill my eyes with tears. How blurry everything gets. Even you get blurry, and the sound of your voice becomes strangely unfamiliar.

Help me to blink away those tears to see that you are standing beside me, wanting to know why I am crying ... wanting to know where it hurts ... wanting to wipe away every tear from my eyes.

Thank you, Jesus, for being there, for never leaving me or forsaking me, even in the darkest and chilliest hours of my life.

Ken Gire

TOWN MOTTOES
Philip Gulley

GOD'S WORD

Be joyful in hope, patient in affliction, faithful in prayer.

Romans 12:12

IN LIEU OF MOUNTAINS and seashores, Indiana has mottoes. Except for my hometown, Danville, which thus far remains motto-free. It isn't because we're without accomplishment—we had the first stoplight in the county—it's because we're a humble people and reluctant to put on airs. Though if we were to brag, we would brag about our town museum, which houses the first postcard ever sent to Danville:

Dear Hobart and Edith, We are fine. How are you? Having a great time. Wish you were here. Love, Clarence and Mary.

PS We think we left the iron plugged in. Could you check it for us?

Our town's Civil War regiment flag is in the museum too. The flag is in pristine condition because the men in our town had a notoriously poor sense of direction and ended up spending the Civil War in Toronto.

Some of the people in Danville are tired of our modesty and are talking about putting up a sign out on Highway 36: *Danville: Home of the Civil War Flag.* Someone ran for the town board as a "sign" candidate, and there's talk of a referendum. The churches are even taking up sides. Pastor Thornburg, over at the Quaker church, has been preaching on the virtues of humility and how Jesus was unpretentious and calls us to be the same, while the Episcopalians have been pouring money into the sign movement. The Baptists have been silent, preferring to carry the banner on weightier matters like salvation by faith and baptism by immersion.

Danville is the county seat for Hendricks County, whose motto is "Garden spot of the world." This is a purely subjective claim and one the rest of the world doesn't necessarily acknowledge. Folks in Switzerland don't look at the Alps and say, "Well, they're pretty, but not as pretty as the strip malls of Hendricks County." The beauty in my hometown isn't in the scenery, but in the people.

Of all the town mottoes in Indiana, I like Swayzee's the most. Their motto is

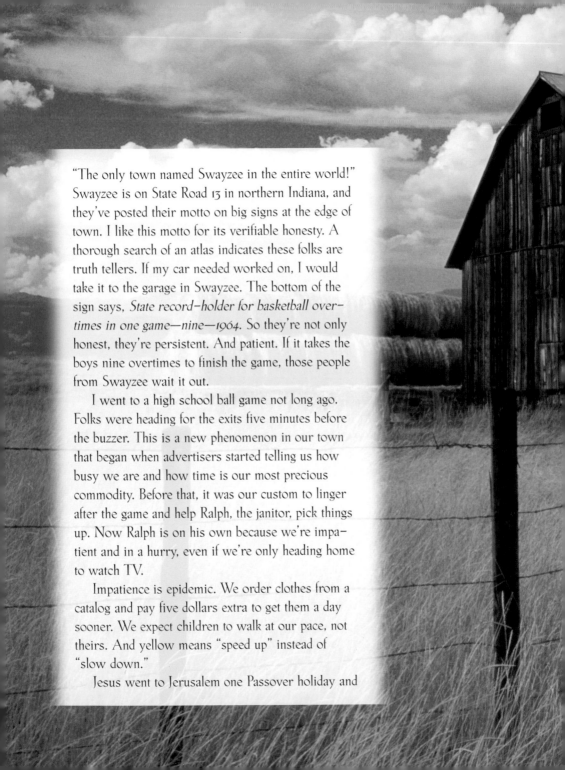

"The only town named Swayzee in the entire world!" Swayzee is on State Road 13 in northern Indiana, and they've posted their motto on big signs at the edge of town. I like this motto for its verifiable honesty. A thorough search of an atlas indicates these folks are truth tellers. If my car needed worked on, I would take it to the garage in Swayzee. The bottom of the sign says, *State record-holder for basketball over-times in one game—nine—1964.* So they're not only honest, they're persistent. And patient. If it takes the boys nine overtimes to finish the game, those people from Swayzee wait it out.

I went to a high school ball game not long ago. Folks were heading for the exits five minutes before the buzzer. This is a new phenomenon in our town that began when advertisers started telling us how busy we are and how time is our most precious commodity. Before that, it was our custom to linger after the game and help Ralph, the janitor, pick things up. Now Ralph is on his own because we're impatient and in a hurry, even if we're only heading home to watch TV.

Impatience is epidemic. We order clothes from a catalog and pay five dollars extra to get them a day sooner. We expect children to walk at our pace, not theirs. And yellow means "speed up" instead of "slow down."

Jesus went to Jerusalem one Passover holiday and

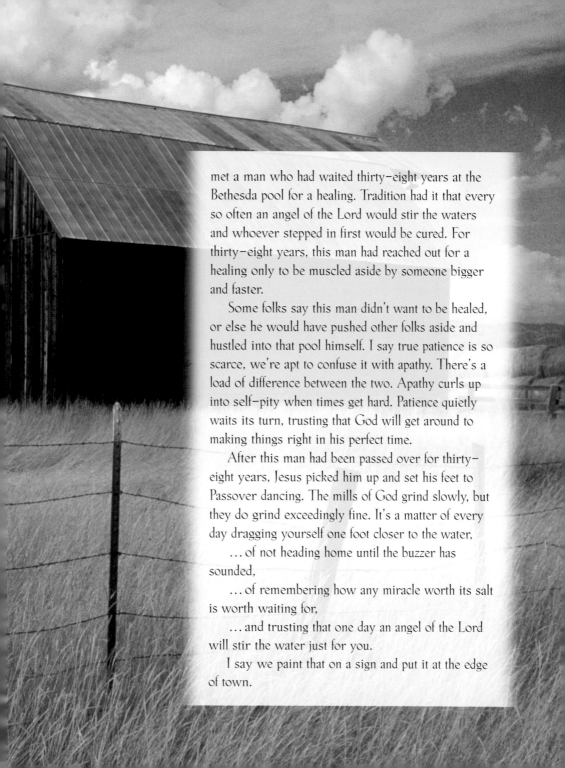

met a man who had waited thirty-eight years at the Bethesda pool for a healing. Tradition had it that every so often an angel of the Lord would stir the waters and whoever stepped in first would be cured. For thirty-eight years, this man had reached out for a healing only to be muscled aside by someone bigger and faster.

Some folks say this man didn't want to be healed, or else he would have pushed other folks aside and hustled into that pool himself. I say true patience is so scarce, we're apt to confuse it with apathy. There's a load of difference between the two. Apathy curls up into self-pity when times get hard. Patience quietly waits its turn, trusting that God will get around to making things right in his perfect time.

After this man had been passed over for thirty-eight years, Jesus picked him up and set his feet to Passover dancing. The mills of God grind slowly, but they do grind exceedingly fine. It's a matter of every day dragging yourself one foot closer to the water,

... of not heading home until the buzzer has sounded,

... of remembering how any miracle worth its salt is worth waiting for,

... and trusting that one day an angel of the Lord will stir the water just for you.

I say we paint that on a sign and put it at the edge of town.

WORDS OF COMFORT

God's care for you goes deeper than your comfort zones. The focus of God's care is your soul. And the expression of his care will be peace and contentment. It's a beautiful promise that reminds you of God's intimate concern whether you're ill for weeks, bedridden for months, or struggling within your marriage for years. Grab hold of that truth and hang on. No matter what.

Joni Eareckson Tada

GOD'S PROMISE

The God of all grace, who called you to his eternal glory in Christ, after you have suffered a little while, will himself restore you and make you strong, firm and steadfast.

1 Peter 5:10

PRAYER

You keep us waiting.
You, the God of all time;
Want us to wait
For the right time in which to discover
Who we are, where we must go,
Who will be with us, and what we must do.

So, thank you . . . for the waiting time.

You keep us looking.
You, the God of all space,
Want us to look in the right and wrong places
For signs of hope,
For people who are hopeless,

For visions of a better world which will appear
Among the disappointments of the world we know.

So, thank you ... for the looking time.

You keep us loving.
You, the God whose name is love,
Want us to be like you—
To love the loveless and the unlovely and the unlovable;
To love without jealousy or design or threat;
And, most difficult of all,
To love ourselves.

So, thank you ... for the loving time.

And in all this,
You keep us.
Through hard questions with no easy answers;
Through failing where we hoped to succeed
And making an impact when we felt we were useless;
Through the patience and the dreams and the love of others;
And through Jesus Christ and his Spirit,
You
Keep us.

So, thank you ... for the keeping time.
        And for now,
        and for ever.

                    John Bell

*D*on't be ashamed of being shattered.

God is looking for broken vessels like

you through whom he can showcase

his splendor. Remember, when it

comes to God's grace, even broken

cups can be filled to overflowing.

JONI EARECKSON TADA

BINDING UP *the* BROKEN-HEARTED

God heals the brokenhearted,
and binds up their wounds.

Psalm 147:3

GOD'S "A" PLAN
Marie Carlson

GOD'S WORD

My frame was not hidden from you
>   when I was made in the secret place.
When I was woven together in the depths of the earth,
>   your eyes saw my unformed body.
All the days ordained for me
>   were written in your book
>   before one of them came to be.

Psalm 139:15–16

I GREW UP IN A CHURCH where people loved me and taught me well about God. So well, in fact, that by the age of thirteen there wasn't a moral dilemma I couldn't have solved with dispatch. Right was white, wrong was black, and what was so hard about that? Things worked in God's system.

It went something like this. In any situation, God always had an "A" plan. If you did the right thing and didn't mess up that plan by sinning, you got to enjoy the corresponding "A" outcome and rewards. However, any major sin altered the "A" plan—God's best—forever. If you failed, the best you could hope for was the "B" or even the "C" plan—God's second or third best. It all made perfect sense … as long as you were, in fact, perfect.

There is almost nothing so certain as the self-righteous knowledge of childhood naiveté—and perhaps, nothing so emotionally lethal as the consequences when it boomerangs. A black-and-white view of God's ways is a soul-shattering experience when one's world changes overnight into impenetrable shades of gray, as mine did when I discovered I was the product of an out-of-wedlock conception.

It was hard enough to accept that my parents hadn't wanted me, the realization that God hadn't wanted me either wounded me beyond articulation. I felt I'd been stamped defective and knocked out of the loop of grace.

I coped at first by striking out at my parents, the violators of the "A" plan. When that didn't work, I retreated, determined to forget by giving the whole thought process cement shoes and tossing it into the backwaters of my soul. And it worked, for a while.

Four years later while a freshman at a Christian college, life came along like Jonah's whale and spit up all the pain I had submerged. No matter what I did that year—good or bad—I felt wrong. I was ambushed by feelings of inadequacy and didn't know why.

Oddly enough, it was a homework assignment that began to salve my soul. One evening, as I was reading the story of Joseph for an Old Testament class, I began to recall all the events and themes of his life—betrayal, slavery, honor, reconciliation. But then a phrase caught my attention. Speaking mercifully to the brothers who had sold him into slavery so many years earlier, Joseph comforts them, saying, "Don't be afraid. Am I in the place of God? You intended to harm me, but God intended it for good to accomplish what is now being done, the saving of many lives" (Genesis 50:19–20).

The words slapped me stone still. I read them again and felt something inside begin to crumble. All the anger and resentment I'd harbored against God for rejecting me as a "B-plan" child came flooding back. Encircling the Bible with my arms, I buried my head on the open pages and wept.

You intended to harm me, but God intended it for good.

That one phrase slaughtered me and saved me at the same time. Destroyed was a skewed view of grace that left no room for the shattering power of God's mercy. Salvaged were the seeds of grace that restored me to my standing as a child of the God who loved me without condition. When my feelings of anger and betrayal rendered me incapable of hearing or talking to God, God sent me Joseph. Joseph redeemed God's identity so that God could begin the work of redeeming mine. Though thousands of years had passed, I was one of the "many lives" Joseph saved. All along, God's "A" plan was redemption, and I qualified; there was no "B" plan.

The beauty and mystery of redemption is this—that I am, and you are, always the most qualified candidate for grace.

WORDS OF COMFORT

Not being welcome is your greatest fear. It connects with your birth fear, your fear of not being welcome in this life, and your death fear, your fear of not being welcome in the life after this. It is the deepseated fear that it would have been better if you had not lived.

Here you are facing the core of the spiritual battle. Are you going to give in to the forces of darkness that say you are not welcome in this life or can you trust the voice of the One who came not to condemn you but to set you free from fear? You have to choose for life. At every moment you have to decide to trust the voice that says, "I love you, I knit you together in your mother's womb" (Psalm 139:13).

Everything Jesus is saying to you can be summarized in the words, "Know that you are welcome." Jesus offers you his own most intimate life with the Father.

Henri J.M. Nouwen

GOD'S PROMISE

Can a mother forget the baby at her breast
    and have no compassion on the child she has borne?
Though she may forget,
    I will not forget you!
See, I have engraved you on the palms of my hands," says the LORD.

Isaiah 49:15–16

PRAYER

Lord Jesus Christ, when I read the gospel stories I am touched by your healing power. You healed sick bodies to be sure, but you did so much more. You healed the spirit and the deep inner mind. Most of all I am touched by your actions of acceptance that spoke healing into those who lived on the margins of life—shoved aside by the strong and powerful.

Speak your healing into me, Lord—body and mind and soul. Most of all, heal my sense of worthlessness. My head tells me that I am of infinite value to you but my heart cannot believe it. Heal my heart, Jesus, heal my heart. Amen.

Richard J. Foster

A LONG NIGHT OF THE SOUL

Krista Brumberg Stevens

GOD'S WORD

We look for light, but all is darkness;
for brightness, but we walk in deep shadows.

Isaiah 59:9

IT HAS BEEN TEN YEARS since my husband, Carl–Eric Wiberg, died from secondary complications of multiple sclerosis just an hour before his twenty–seventh birthday. And what a long ten years it has been.

Looking back, I can now agree with C.S. Lewis that sorrow is a process, not a state. But mine began with a "long night of the soul" where God was absent, far away, or at worst, uncaring or even non–existent. I screamed, ranted, raved, and threw my pain up into the universe where it ricocheted against the silent stars and returned like a boomerang to slice up my heart into more little pieces.

And then my heart turned to stone. I hated God. I also found it difficult to live without a heart. My skin felt like it had been turned inside out and could no longer protect me from the searing pain of a gentle touch. The last thing I wanted, or believed in, was hope or healing. For me, the tragedy was not Carl's death, but my survival.

I can remember being drawn, almost against my will, back to church about a year and a half after Carl's death. I found an old church, white with blue doors, that sat looking over a harbor. Inside, tall rectangular windows let in the sea light that streamed over white painted pews. When I attended, which was sporadically, I sat in the far back. I chose my seat carefully for two reasons.

The first had to do with the windows. From one window I could see the steeple of a nearby church and from another window I could see a tree and the top of a red building. The rest showed only the sky and the strange and beautiful light of the ocean reflecting the sun's rays up into the atmosphere.

The door was another reason I sat toward the rear. It was comforting to know there was a quick exit. I was afraid to sit too near the altar. I didn't want to get closer to God. Even sitting in the last pew with my spine pressed against the back of the wooden pew was dangerous. I had been burned by God once before and I didn't want to get burned again.

Besides, the light from God was too bright for me, still ensconced in the shadow of pain and death. It hurt, that light, the same burning light that caused Moses to avert his face. He was no fool; he knew the power and heat of a thousand burning suns in that bush could reduce him to a smidgen of ash in a second. I knew that too.

So for a long time I sat in the back of the church and spent most of the time looking out the windows. The minister's voice was as soothing as a warm comforter on the sharp, jagged angles of my loss, but I didn't hear his words. It was almost too much just to sit there in the presence of a God who I felt had abandoned me in my hour of need.

I sat there through the seasons. The tree transformed from a black scratch against a low, white sky to an explosion of green buds and then into an emerald canopy against a cobalt blue sky. Then in the fall, the golden leaves swirled up into the heavens with the eastward wind and simply, silently, and slowly the snow began to fall.

I'm the last one to promise that time heals all wounds, and I'm not even sure that's true or that I want that to happen. But, as recorded in Ecclesiastes 3, there is a time for everything. For me, there was a time to return to God and that's why I went and sat in the back of the church. I didn't receive any holy answers or sacred explanations. Honestly, I'm not sure there are any or that I would have accepted them. But I returned, regardless. Like Dylan Thomas, I had "raged against the dying of the light" until my voice was hoarse, my body weary, and my mind and soul a soggy gray mess.

There were many times as I sat there in that church by the sea that I struggled to keep the tears from falling, sometimes successfully, sometimes not. But

there in that wonderful church with the light from the windows streaming down upon my head, I began to grow stronger.

The scars of my loss will never be completely healed but I have turned to the light. I have affirmed that my life is bound up in God. I have brought the most precious parts of my life to be blessed by him. In that same church with the windows reaching up to the heavens, I remarried. Three years later on a Costa Rican beach in bright morning light, my son was dedicated. I have come forward to stand in the light, knowing my shadows are on the edge, knowing life is hard, but knowing that God is still there and that it is my choice where I choose to stand. Grief is a process. But in that process we are offered options. The choices are never easy. I choose to sit in the streams of light and I choose to let someone wrap his arms around me and give me a child. And I choose to remember Carl and the happiness we had for a few short years.

As Carl's father said as we walked away from his snow-covered grave, "May God bless you and keep you and make his face to shine upon you." Amen.

WORDS OF COMFORT

The great spiritual call of the Beloved Children of God is to pull their brokenness away from the shadow of the curse and put it under the light of the blessing.... When we keep listening attentively to the voice calling us the Beloved, it becomes possible to live our brokenness, not as a confirmation of our fear that we are worthless, but as an opportunity to purify and deepen the blessing that rests upon us.... Great and heavy burdens become light and easy when they are lived in the light of the blessing. What seemed intolerable becomes a challenge. What seemed a reason for depression becomes a source of purification. What seemed punishment becomes a gentle pruning. What seemed rejection becomes a way to a deeper communion.

Henri J.M. Nouwen

GOD'S PROMISE

God is light; in him there is no darkness at all.

1 John 1:5

PRAYER

Ah, Lord, to whom all hearts are open, you can pilot the ship of our souls far better than we can. Stand up, Lord, and command the stormy wind and the troubled sea of our hearts to be still, and at peace in you, so that we may look up to you undisturbed, and rest in union with you, our Lord. Do not let us be carried hither and thither by wandering thoughts, but, forgetting all else, let us see and hear you alone. Renew our spirits; kindle in us your light, that it may shine within us, and our hearts may burn in love and adoration for you. Let your Holy Spirit dwell in us continually, and make us your temples and sanctuary. Fill us with divine love and light and life, with devout and heavenly thoughts, with comfort and strength, with joy and peace. Amen.

Johann Arndt

A Season for Sorrow
Maxine Dowd Jensen

God's Word

Blessed are those who mourn, for they will be comforted.

Matthew 5:4

IT ISN'T EASY TO WATCH a man die slowly. Nor is it easy when his life is suddenly cut off. Either way, if you are the wife, you die, too. I did. Oh, I was still breathing, walking, talking. But I wasn't living. I did the usual things one does at a time like that. I contacted the church, hired the undertaker, and selected the casket. It should have helped that the undertaker was a friend and that my pastor had known me since my late teens. But it did not help. I was alone.

All of the things I had to do, I did. All of the family members who helped and the friends who pressed my hand and murmured words of sympathy and assurance were appreciated. Yet—I was alone. More alone than ever before.

The numbness that follows parting can continue for an indefinite period. I broke through that numbness to life and living again when I remembered....

I remembered that October day when we went to Maple Lake. At first I sat in the car. I watched him start walking toward the water's edge. Something about the droop of his shoulders stirred my heart and I knew that, though it was chilly, I needed to go with him. Quickly, I caught up. We linked our hands and scuffed our feet through the fallen leaves.

I stole a glance at him. The only man I had ever loved. *What were his thoughts?* The usual happy smile and light in his eyes were missing. Had he been thinking, as I, that this was his last look at autumn?

Suddenly the wind forced its chill through my sweater to my heart. The first chill of winter. *And of death?* Our fingers gently touched, then clasped together tightly. As if this touch, this grasp, would hold us together—forever.

Slowly we walked back to the car. We sat there for a time—watching the wind play with the leaves—noting the sun's fading rays catch every color. Our hands and arms were still entwined. But I dared not look. I dared not find in his eyes what I

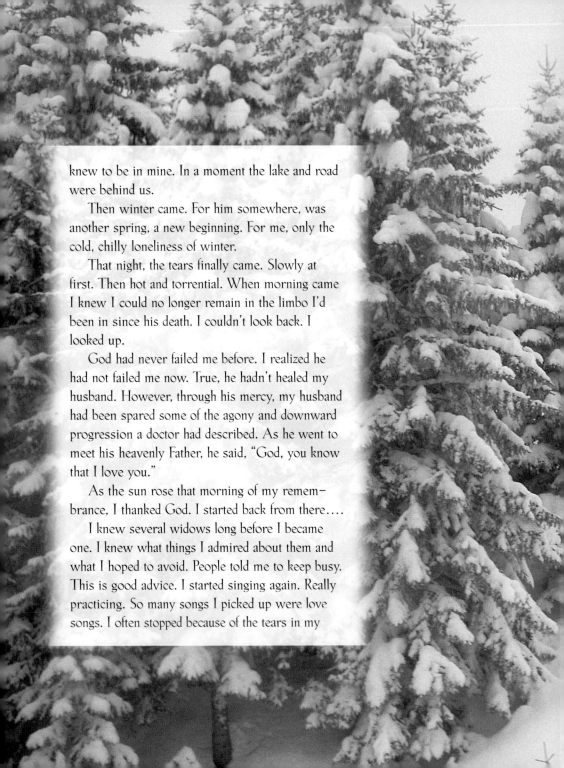

knew to be in mine. In a moment the lake and road were behind us.

Then winter came. For him somewhere, was another spring, a new beginning. For me, only the cold, chilly loneliness of winter.

That night, the tears finally came. Slowly at first. Then hot and torrential. When morning came I knew I could no longer remain in the limbo I'd been in since his death. I couldn't look back. I looked up.

God had never failed me before. I realized he had not failed me now. True, he hadn't healed my husband. However, through his mercy, my husband had been spared some of the agony and downward progression a doctor had described. As he went to meet his heavenly Father, he said, "God, you know that I love you."

As the sun rose that morning of my remembrance, I thanked God. I started back from there....

I knew several widows long before I became one. I knew what things I admired about them and what I hoped to avoid. People told me to keep busy. This is good advice. I started singing again. Really practicing. So many songs I picked up were love songs. I often stopped because of the tears in my

eyes and the lump in my throat.

I'm writing again. Something I did successfully before marriage. It's fun. It consumes some time.

Still there are periods of idleness, of sleepless-ness. Periods when once again I "wait upon the Lord" and discover—as promised in Isaiah—that my strength is renewed. But waiting isn't easy. Often we must wait, for guidance and help. I try.

I also try to spend some of my alone time in meditation, in reading inspirational books, in trying to understand God's book, in prayer. I tell him the problems and needs of my friends. I ask advice on both big and little matters. Sometimes sad and disturbing thoughts crowd in. But I find that being alone gives me a chance to plan my future.

My widowed friends tell me it gets worse, not better, as time goes by. They may be right and I may be a "cockeyed optimist." However, with God, all things are possible and I'm expecting—and receiving—a rewarding future.

There is a future for a widow. There is access to wisdom and guidance through God. There is still the possibility of happiness—even for a widow.

I can't know about you, but I'm a widow who keeps looking up.

WORDS OF COMFORT

If you have lost someone—through death,
divorce, broken communications, or whatever the
reason—and you are dwelling only in the past,
you are watering, fertilizing, and cultivating a
decaying seed. No fresh green plant for future
harvest will grow from that. If you are to turn
your hurts into healing, you must do all you can
to help the seeds of past blessings germinate and
grow toward a harvest of future blessings.

V. Gilbert Beers

GOD'S PROMISE

"For I know the plans I have for you," declares
the LORD, "plans to prosper you and not to harm
you, plans to give you hope and a future."

Jeremiah 29:11

PRAYER

Take one moment of my life, Lord,
on to your cross.
Draw it into the dark forge of your love;
So that, broken,
healed,
transfigured,
cleansed,
reborn,
it may be lived,
even yet,
in praise.

ACKNOWLEDGEMENTS

The publisher has made every effort to trace the ownership of all quotations and to request the appropriate permissions. In the event of a question arising from the use of a quotation, we regret any error made and will be pleased to make the necessary correction in future editions of this book.

Adam, David. *A Desert in the Ocean.* Copyright 2000 by David Adam. Published by Paulist Press.

Arndt, Johann. Excerpted from *2000 Years of Prayer,* compiled by Michael John Radford Counsell. Copyright 1995 by SPCK. Published in the USA by Morehouse Publishing.

Arthur, Kay. *Lord, I Want to Know You.* Copyright 1992 by Kay Arthur. Published by Multnomah Publishers.

Austin, John. Excerpted from *The Complete Book of Christian Prayer.* Copyright 1995 SPCK. Published in 1998 in the USA by The Continuum Publishing Company.

Barclay, William. *Prayers for the Christian Year.* Copyright 1964 by SCM Press Ltd. Published by SCM Press Ltd.

Beers, V. Gilbert. *Finding Purpose in Your Pain.* Copyright 1988 by V. Gilbert Beers. Published by Fleming H. Revell.

Bell, John. Excerpted from *The Complete Book of Christian Prayer.* Copyright 1995 SPCK. Published in 1998 in the USA by The Continuum Publishing Company.

Bloss, Joanna. Originally published in the February 1999 issue of *The Covenant Companion.*

Brumberg Stevens, Krista. Originally published in the July 1994 issue of *The Covenant Companion.*

Buechner, Frederick. *The Magnificent Defeat.* Copyright 1985 by Frederick Buechner. Used by permission of HarperCollins Publishers.

Carlson, Marie. Used by permission of the author.

Cassiday, Sheila. Excerpted from *Laughter, Silence and Shouting.* Copyright 1994 by Kathy Keay. Used by permission of HarperCollins Publishers.

Collins, Aileen. Used by permission of the author.

Crabb, Larry. *Connecting.* Copyright 1997 by Larry Crabb. Published by Word Publishing. *The Safest Place on Earth.* Copyright 1999 by Larry Crabb. Published by Word Publishing.

Curtis Higgs, Liz. *Mirror, Mirror on the Wall, Have I Got News for You.* Copyright 1997 by Liz Curtis Higgs. Published by Thomas Nelson Publishers.

Dowd Jensen, Maxine. Originally published in the January/February 1997 issue of *Virtue* magazine.

Foster, Richard J. *Prayer.* Copyright 1992 by Richard J. Foster. Used by permission of HarperCollins Publishers.

Gassett, Donna. Originally published in the September 7, 1994 issue of *Alliance Life.*

Gulley, Philip. *Home Town Tales.* Copyright 1998 by Philip Gulley. Published by Multnomah Publishers.

Guthrie, Stan. Originally published in the November/December 1998 issue of *Moody.*

Habermann, Johann. Excerpted from *The Complete Book of Christian Prayer.* Copyright 1995 SPCK. Published in 1998 in the USA by The Continuum Publishing Company.

Hanlin, Polly. Originally published as "Encounter in the Laundromat," in the Spring 1999 issue of *Faith at Work.*

Harter, Marguerite. Originally published in the July/August 1997 issue of *Virtue.*

Leno, Patty. Originally published in the September 7, 1994 issue of *Alliance Life.*

Lucco, Richard B. Originally published in the May 1998 issue of *The Covenant Companion.*

Used by permission of Zondervan